WHY I AM NOT A BUS DRIVER

Ashley Hickson-Lovence is the author of *The 392*, *Your Show* and *Wild East*—overall winner of the East Anglian Book Awards 2024. He has a PhD in Creative and Critical Writing from the University of East Anglia. His nominations include the Black Excellence Award for Outstanding Contribution to Literature 2023 and the Carnegie Medal for Writing 2025. *Why I Am Not a Bus Driver* is his first poetry collection.

BY THE SAME AUTHOR

Wild East
(Penguin, 2024)

Your Show
(Faber & Faber, 2022)

The 392
(OWN IT!, 2019)

Why I Am Not a Bus Driver

ASHLEY HICKSON-LOVENCE

BAD BETTY PRESS

First published in 2025 by Bad Betty Press
Cobden Place, Cobden Chambers, Nottingham NG1 2ED

badbettypress.com

Copyright ©Ashley Hickson-Lovence 2025

Ashley Hickson-Lovence has asserted his right to be identified as the author of this work in accordance with Section 77 of the Copyright, Designs and Patents Act of 1988.

PB ISBN: 978-1-913268-74-9
EPUB ISBN: 978-1-913268-75-6

A CIP record of this book is available from the British Library.

Copyright of cover and interior images is with the author
Book design by Amy Acre

Printed and bound in the UK by TJ Books Limited, Padstow, Cornwall
using FSC® Certified paper from responsibly managed forests

For Alister Hickson

CONTENTS

I. AMH

Greenford Avenue	17
Heathrow	18
Morne Rouge (Dr Death Is Dead)	21
Peterborough Station (Rail Replacement: I'm a Train Choo Choo)	25
Ring Road	26
Beechwood Avenue	27
Gunnersbury Cemetery	28
Ealing (Half Marathon)	31
Southall	35
Liverpool Street	36
Eastmead Avenue	37
Our Lady of the Visitation Catholic Church (Grandad's Hands)	38
Thickthorn	41
Great Ormond Street	42
Glastonbury	45
Shampoo Poem	46
Beechwood Avenue II	47
Beechwood Avenue III (Grandfather Clock Poem)	51
Glastonbury II	52
Birkbeck Avenue	55
Munster Road	56
Notting Hill	59
Ketchup Poem	63

Homes Under the Hammer Poem	64
Norwich South Recycling Centre	66
Burger King Poem	69
Heaven	70

II. "THE FAMOUS 7A"

Heathfield	77
Imperial War Museum	79
Duxford	81
Whittlesford Parkway	83
Hinxton	85
Pampisford	86
Sawston	87

III. AFTER FRANK

Upper Tulse Hill	91
Angel	92
Marriott's Way	93
Clinger Court	94
Highbury Barn (the 263 has been extended!)	95
Why I Am Not a Bus Driver	96
Acknowledgements	98

Why I Am Not a Bus Driver

When the genie comes out, wish for late buses
and missed trains, and beers on benches,
because when someone is gone, they are gone.

—Kareem Parkins-Brown

At night on the dock
the buses glow like
clouds and I am lonely
thinking of flutes

—Frank O'Hara, 'Morning'

I.
AMH

GREENFORD AVENUE

Good with our hands but in very different ways,
I wouldn't know where to start under
the bonnet of a broken-down car
or changing a flat tyre and you wouldn't
understand the point of me writing these poems
but I remember you tightening the bolts of the bike
you bought me on Greenford Avenue
so we could ride round the houses like the E10
and later that evening before Dad came
to pick me up and drop me back at Mum's,
your grease-stained fingers slipping me a twenty
or two which you told me to put in my pocket
straight away just in case I wouldn't feel
the warmth of those crisp notes again.

HEATHROW

So you want to be a paddy?
was one of the last things you said to me
over the phone when I told you I was
applying for my Irish passport.
I'm doing it for Nanny I snapped
and today looking up thinking back to when we used
to take the 105 to Heathrow on Sundays sometimes
to see the planes taking off as I
prepare to sell the little Peugeot you left me
with the private number plate I was keen to keep
and the smell of you lingering in the fabric of the seats
but it's OK because there are always buses
and planes taking off again and again
soaring further and further into the distance.

MORNE ROUGE (DR DEATH IS DEAD)

He had a good innings is what I keep
saying to describe your passing.
You didn't even like cricket that much
for a West Indian of your generation.
You were a wrestler, *Dr Death* your stage name.
We made plans to go to Grenada one day,
you said you would pay for my flight
and I would just need spending money
and now as the weather turns big-coat cold
I've been thinking about what could have been,
you and me sinking bottles of Carib on Morne Rouge,
the silver of our rings clinking against the glass
instead of stuck here wrestling with something
hard to pin down, grapple, hold, grasp.

PETERBOROUGH STATION (RAIL REPLACEMENT: I'M A TRAIN CHOO CHOO)

You must have been a bit shit, I think,
weighing up my options at a sodden Peterborough Station.
There's a signalling problem at Ely
and all the trains to Norwich are delayed.
There was that time you mentioned another woman,
I think you even showed us a picture.
She was beautiful. Welsh too you said proudly
to my future wife, a bit Welsh herself,
who you were meeting for the first time.
She looked at it, you and then glared at me.
And I'm here still stranded trying not to entertain
the possibility you would do that to Nanny
while waiting for a rail replacement bus
that probably won't ever come.

RING ROAD

Before you left, you left a couple of your
rings for me, both had seen better days,
both in need of a good clean. One engraved
'AH' and the other a proper chunky signet,
its face carved into the shape of a steel pan.
I've always been painfully ashamed of my nail-
bitten fingers but I've always loved my bling.
Like a gram of old gear, I keep the pair of them
in a little plastic pouch in the top drawer
in my study. Don't think they're worth much,
the silver quality is questionable. I should
take them to the jewellers, get them fixed,
but I worry they are too large to resize,
the hole too big to shrink.

BEECHWOOD AVENUE

It's New Year's Eve, your birthday,
and I've spent most of it working on a new novel
that's sort of based on the life of the man
you didn't even know existed until about
five years before your death when you found that letter.

> *Hi mother, I have left things for so long hoping
> that you may change your mind about meeting me.*

Nanny had hidden the letter, tucked it away,
then died six months later. We had no idea.
None of us. The first time you met her other son
I wasn't there, but I saw the light
in your eyes in the picture on Facebook.
Maybe in his face you saw her smile again.

GUNNERSBURY CEMETERY

Again I wake up in the red, poet poor
with this belly-rumbling desire to be a bus driver.
To march over to the garage,
sign on the dotted line, hand in the
HMRC and Equal Opportunities forms,
then drive a double decker down the M11
to pick you up on Beechwood Avenue.
We'd whizz by your favourite haunts:
first to the bookies on Lady Margaret Road
then down to Heathrow to see the planes,
Shepherds Bush for popcorn and patties
before terminating at Gunnersbury Cemetery,
where I'd drop you off next to Nanny
for a well-deserved break.

EALING (HALF MARATHON)

It's Sunday, a few months after her death,
and I'm at the start line of the Ealing Half Marathon
wearing a vest with her face on for the both of us.
Rain isn't forecast but you've got your brolly to lean on
while you wait for me to weave round
the backstreets of the borough and back again.
At the gun I start strong snaking off course
running my own route down memory lane:
left where you bought me a matching Claddagh ring
from the jewellers on the Broadway.
Left towards Castle Bar Park, then left to London Fields
for my book launch (I'm so glad you made it)
left and left and left again

                          until it starts to feel right.

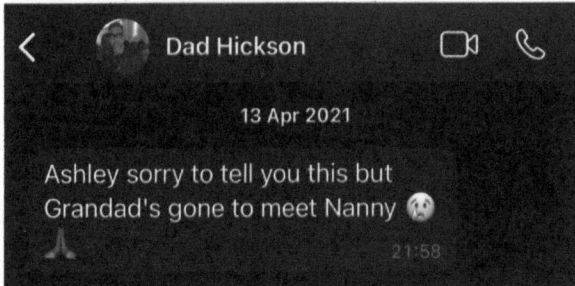

SOUTHALL

I always worried when you went
on one of your Sunday bus rides
wearing all your bling, especially
after you told me someone at a
bus stop in Southall approached you once
admiring your crucifix trying to
sweet-talk it into their back pocket.
A chancer who saw the sparkle of the silver—
felt the weight of it—and the umbrella you used
as a walking stick on the sunniest of days
before they clocked the firm fists of your past:
the wrestling, the fixing of things, the no-nonsense parenting.
I had nothing to worry about in the end.
You died with it close it your chest.

LIVERPOOL STREET

Two tooled-up teenagers on a moped
taught me the word agoraphobia.
My therapist later confirmed it.
But today I'm putting on my bravest face for your funeral.
We stop just short of Liverpool Street
while the train waits for a free platform.
For a moment we're suspended, stationary
next to these big billboards with every flag of the world on it.
My carriage stops directly opposite
the colours of Grenada while *I'll Be Missing You*
turns to Arrow's *Long Time* in my ears.
I could cry but I want to dance
and I don't need fancy poetry right now,
just normal words, please, to slowly move on.

EASTMEAD AVENUE

On the day of your funeral I met mum and we took
the Central Line to your house and the nearer
we got the more uncomfortable it felt because
I was on these nutty meds that made my piss red
and I was bursting by the time we got to yours
and the house was full of people I only half recognised,
which felt strange in a way I couldn't put my finger on
and the flush of the toilet was broken, blocked,
I needed to go badly but my piss would look like blood
so I went round the back by Eastmead Avenue
where the council had fenced off both ends
of the alleyway I had hoped to use so I just
had to wait, hold it in. You bet by the time
we got to the church it all came gushing out.

OUR LADY OF THE VISITATION CATHOLIC CHURCH (GRANDAD'S HANDS)

after Bill Withers' 'Grandma's Hands'

Grandad's hands were made in Grenada
Grandad's hands worked the land he used to say
Grandad's hands held on tight boarding for Britain
Grandad's hands wrinkled washing dishes for pennies
Grandad's hands beat pan so well, call it *callus calypso*
Grandad's hands were good at fixing things
Grandad's hands polka-dotted with oil spots
Grandad's hands did paperwork on the dinner table
with half an eye on *Emmerdale*
Grandad's hands drove me slowly back the station
Grandad's hands skinnier than I remember
clasped in the casket years of grafting paid for
Grandad's hands are more than just the subject of this poem
they steeple straight up towards the sky.

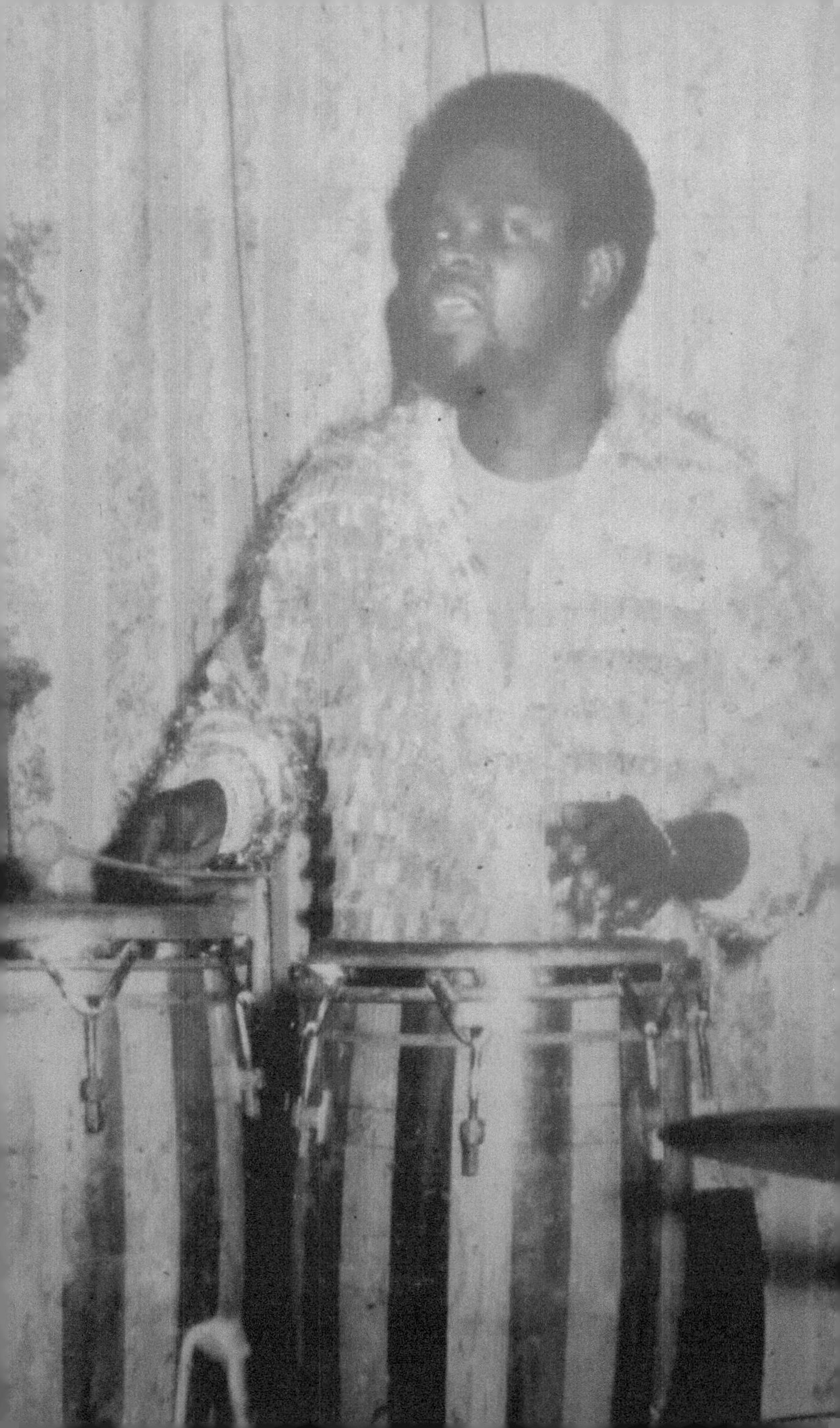

THICKTHORN

big up the 149   big up the 25   big up the 242   big up
the W5   big up the P4   big up the E10   big up
The 392   big up the little Peugeot you left me
which I drove back to Norwich the evening after your
funeral   it reeked of you   making it harder
to concentrate   already drained   flat-tyre
tired   PSI half of what it should be   couldn't work the
high beams   so when I was diverted off the A11
I couldn't really see   lurched around shadowy country
lanes   squinting down at the satnav   cars too
close behind   *why are headlights getting brighter?*
        managing somehow to turn just in time around
every curve & corner   it would have been some sick
irony if I died the day of your funeral driving your old
car   but I made it to Thickthorn   made it to the
safety of McDonald's   pulled into the drive-
thru & thankfully   the chips were hot & crunchy
reminding me how delicious it is to still be alive

GREAT ORMOND STREET

Survived nigger-hunting Teddy Boys in the fifties.
Married Nanny. Two kids. Two houses.
Mainly a mechanic, but for a brief spell
in the late eighties a lollipop man,
made it into the paper raising funds for Great Ormond Street.
In your later years, no longer stopping traffic,
started spotting a sprinkling of skin tags
sprouting all over your neck, face, eyelids.
Blossoming black moles. Plucky little dots.
I've got a few myself and tried to pick them off at first,
scratch them off like a scab and wait to bleed to death.
Used to think they were little full stops
but now I see them more as an ellipsis,
like there's still so much more of the story to tell.

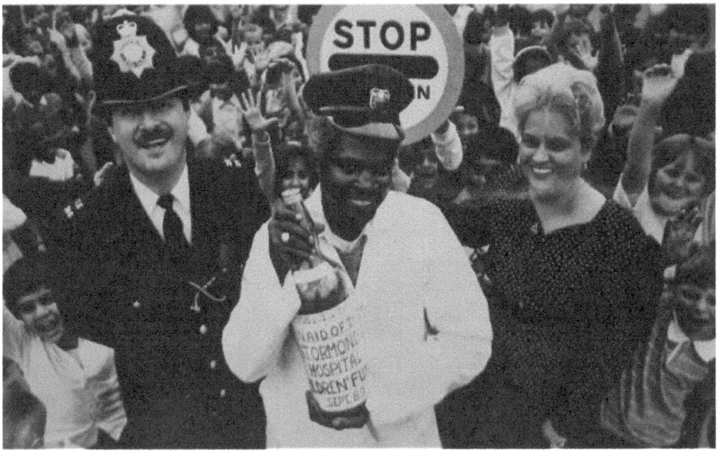
STOP

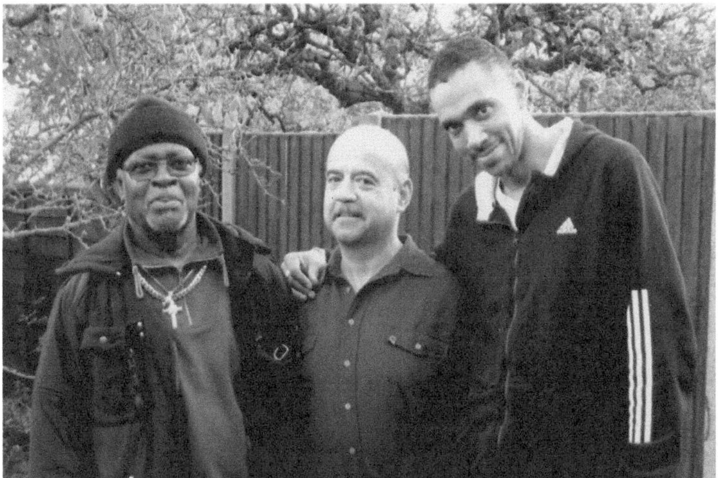

GLASTONBURY

This morning I tumbled into a Hot Chip rabbit hole
Ready For The Floor, Boy From School, Over and Over.
Next is a live performance of *I Feel Better*
from their 2010 set at Glastonbury.
Lead singer Alexis wears a silly glittery hat.
They play alongside a band called Steel Harmony
and there's something about that familiar twinkling sound
of stick hitting pan that instantly reminds me of your hands
and spontaneous practice sessions in the garage
and I'm imagining it's you playing in front of thousands
and as Alexis sings and Joe on backing vocals messes up a bit
I'm on the sofa skanking out watching you on stage
dancing and playing and smiling
and I feel better. I feel better. I feel

SHAMPOO POEM

Every time I wash my hair
the smell of Neutrogena t/gel therapeutic
anti-dandruff medicated shampoo
Neutar™ solubilised coal tar extract
for itchy and flaky scalp
for the treatment of psoriasis
and seborrheic dermatitis (250ml)
reminds me of you and the
greasy tools kept in your garage.
It's not working. I still have a flaky scalp
and I'm too embarrassed to go to
the barbers most weeks but at least, every few days,
I have the memory of you making things better
lingering right here at the top of my head.

BEECHWOOD AVENUE II

The video flickers. AV1 in the corner.
Colourful floral cushions. Knitted sofa covers
like a tea cosy or a football net.
Thick orange curtain blocks out Beechwood Avenue
as you shuffle into shot. The white of your smile
brighter than the collar of your shirt.
You sit. Lean back. But something isn't right.
You get up. Readjust the camera. Sit back down.   Nope.
You come closer. Tip it a bit. Tease it into position.
You've got it. You settle into your seat and
after a brief pause start your rendition
of Don McLean's *And I Love You* with a smile
bigger than the moon. Holder of notes.
Music in your bones. *And I love you so*

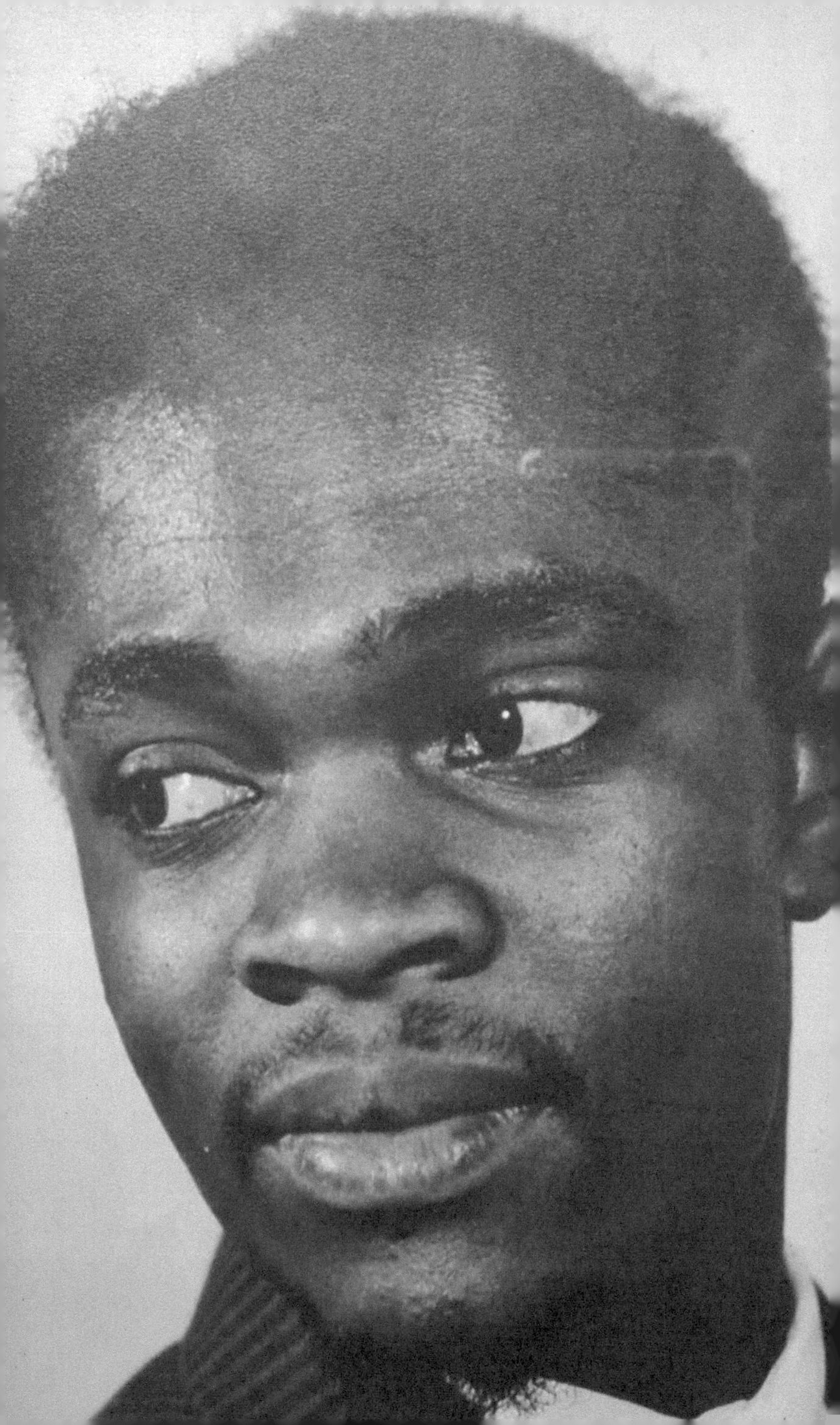

BEECHWOOD AVENUE III
(GRANDFATHER CLOCK POEM)

The clock's not working like it should so you
take it down to have a look. It tells the time
but doesn't chime so you tinker with it
like a seasoned surgeon while I scrawl
in my A-Z, making up new routes
with a highlighter. I never got why
there was no E4 so I write to the garage
on Greenford Road with suggestions
and hand-drawn maps. They never listen
but do send me a keyring once, and a pen.
And all these years later Dad has sold
the house on Beechwood Avenue and bought
a new one down in Kent and I'm still writing
about buses wondering where *does* the time go.

GLASTONBURY II

inspired by Soft Play's Glastonbury 2024
performance of 'Everything and Nothing'

I want more of that mandolin please
tattooed and topless screaming a timely
first line about bombs dropping
to fearless fans hoisted high by
the hands of strangers and watch
them surf towards the stage
I want flags to be waved
I want everyone to know *I miss you everyday*
I want them to sing and shout
while others just mumble along
I want you to know that I love you I love you I love you
and by the end of the song
I want to look out into the heart of the crowd
glassy-eyed, knowing I've done you proud

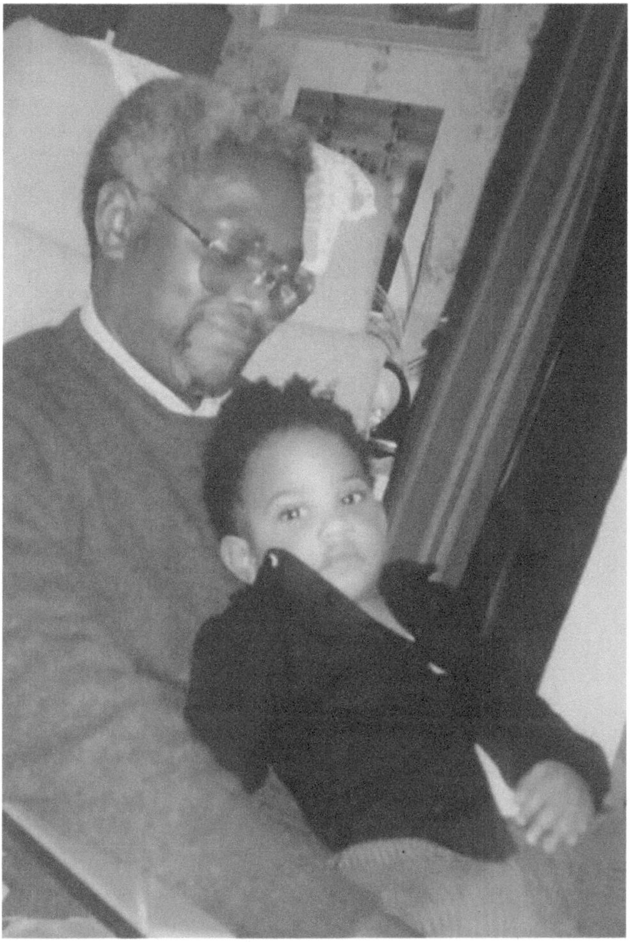

BIRKBECK AVENUE

I was embarrassed that time you came
to watch me referee on Birkbeck Avenue.
You stood on the sidelines and your grimace
gave away the ache in your knees
and I still pretended you weren't there.
It wasn't a big game but I wanted
the players to think I was in control.
I wanted to give the impression I wasn't someone
who's too scared to leave the house most days
and has to sink two tins of something to
quash the nerves of being on my way somewhere.
At the final whistle, hobbling towards you,
I wanted to look like someone who didn't need as
much support as he actually did and still does.

MUNSTER ROAD

Grenada's Lord Kitchener / London was the place for
you whether they liked it or not / ship docker / door
knocker / hotel dish washer / stacking them Ps like
clean plates / chasing the British dream / Grenada's
Sam Selvon / lonely Londoner but not for long /
donned denim back home so refuse to wear it here /
it's a suit & tie ting soon as your shift ends / go meet a
friend / head west first to your flat in Fulham / looking
smoking while smoking / Grenada's Rudolph Walker /
Love Thy Neighbour / can see what Nanny saw / for
sure / from the top floor / her sharp-dressed saviour
/ devoutly tight-lipped / so much she didn't say /
couldn't admit / hid / before pulling an Irish goodbye
/ leaving you behind / Grenada's Sir Trevor McDonald
/ News at Ten watcher / mechanic / wrestler / lollipop
man / father / fudge-buyer / musician / listen /
Mac Miller said *music is a beautiful thing* / & he was
right / that's why I'm *always* tap tap tapping / fingers
on keyboard / pen to table / TV remote on knee /
air drumming to the beat / listening to bangers &
imagining I'm the frontman / following in your fat
footsteps / yellow-soled & fleshy / ankles bulging /
bulbous & swollen / years of keeping rhythm taking its
toll on your toes / your hypertensive heart / socialising
takes practice & I'm tiring / but still writing & writing
& writing

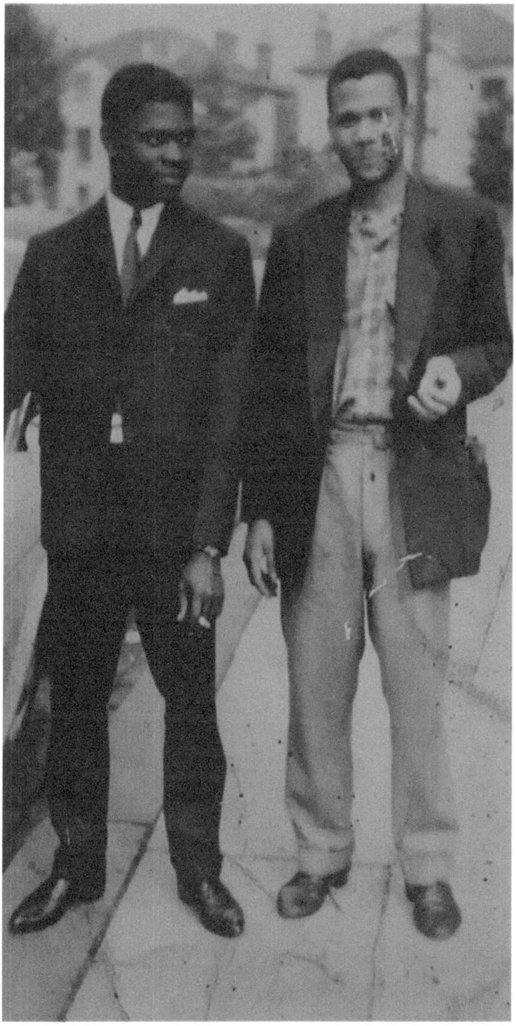

NOTTING HILL

bop through / shimmy past a bodypopping fed / might
be from East originally but I know these streets / went
college round the corner / they can't move all this to a
park / scale it down / kettle us in / you wouldn't have
it / & I know you're up there shaking a leg / as you did
regularly since 66 / you loved it here / gem studded
your creps / wrists greased / primed & ready to beat
pan / this is our annual musical protest / yes / being
streetwise is key / same as at Glastonbury / so we keep
it moving / shuffle past a taser-eyed officer / the one
catching a whine who's probably gone viral already /
who glares at me / all straight like a baton / when all
I want to do is two-step with you on these same streets
again

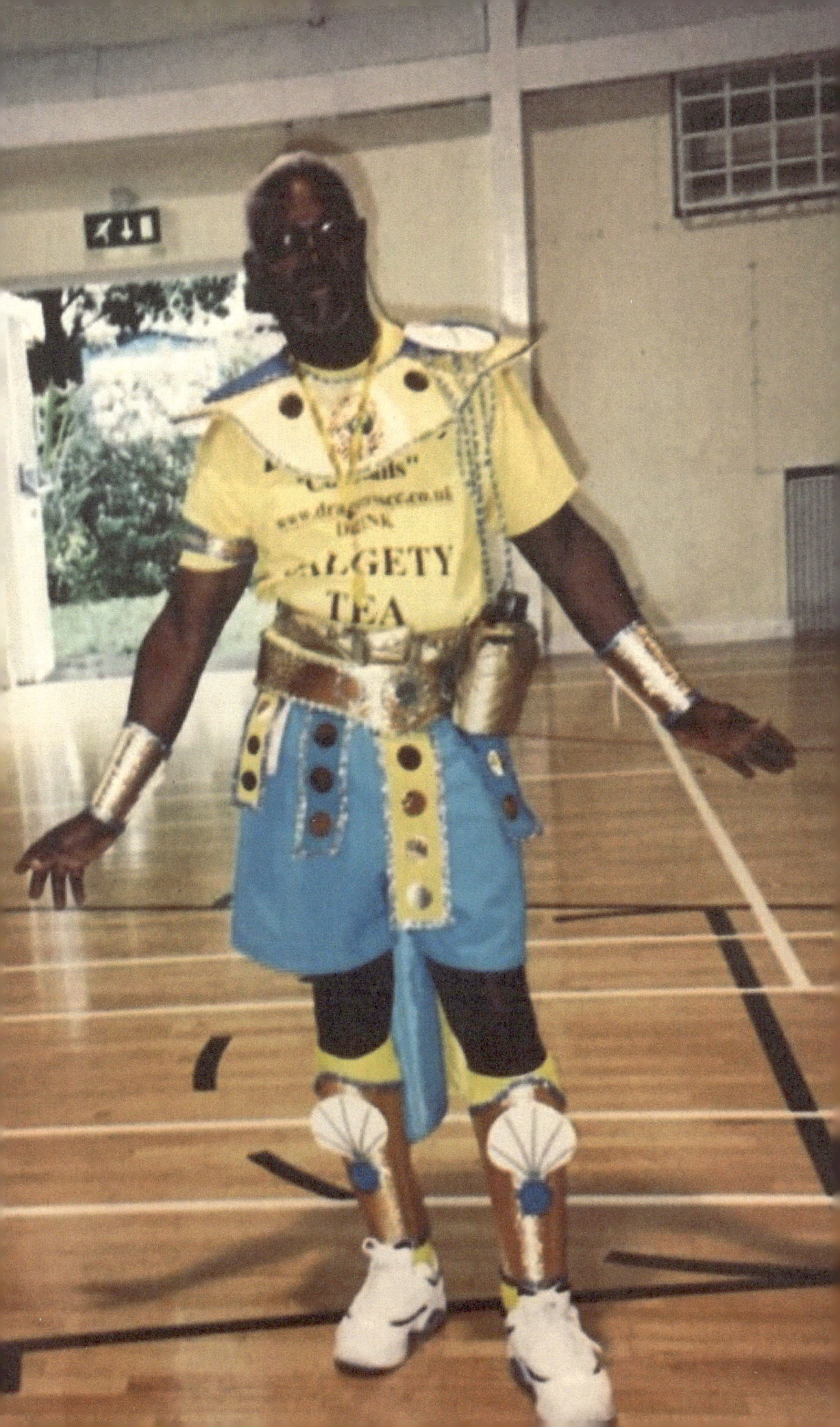
TEA

KETCHUP POEM

I know I should have visited more,
anxiety or not, I could have at least
answered your calls.
Spent ages deleting all the
notifications from our WhatsApp chat.
When I did come round,
you used to warm up Tesco
sausage rolls for me knowing I
would miss the routine of having something
in my belly like when Nanny was around.
But the ketchup you dug out
from the cupboard in the kitchen
was long out of date. It always was.
We tried to move on but everything was off.

HOMES UNDER THE HAMMER POEM

look at the music
the sitting room smells of Ceefax
feels like a throwback
no Sky or WiFi
just the sound of Homes Under the Hammer
I've done the research
viewed the property
read the legal pack
I call Twitter 'X' now
but I still regret wanting to look
as white as Nanny once when I was younger.
I've got the life I've always wanted
but still feel destructive enough
to want to start all over

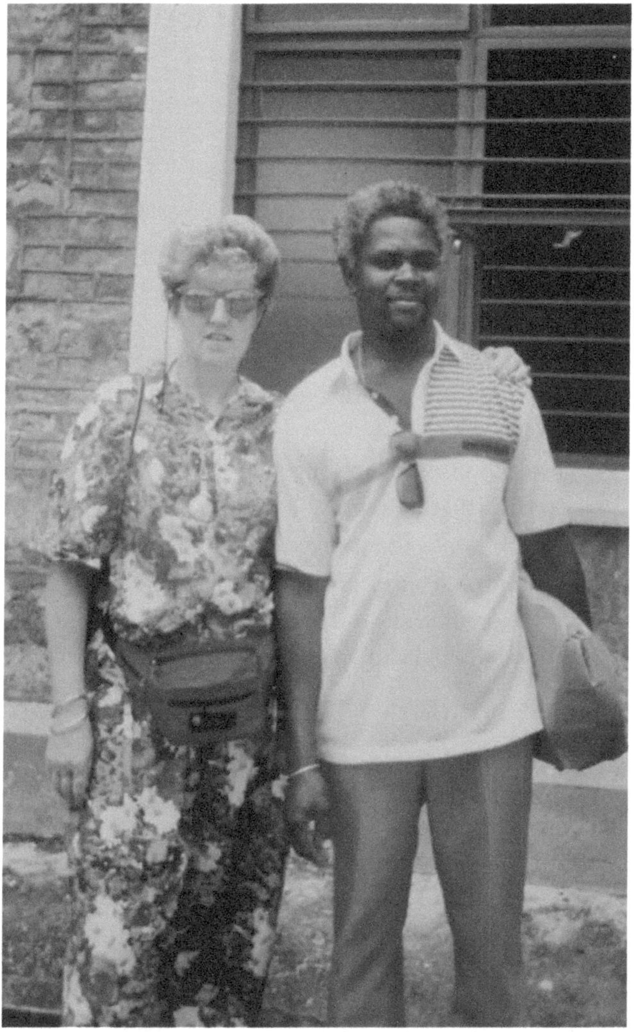

NORWICH SOUTH RECYCLING CENTRE

Last week clearing out the garage
I find a box of things from the Peugeot:
de-icer, WD40, screenwash, a dead torch.
We load it into the boot of our new car
but at the tip, just about to chuck it,
we are stopped by an old man in orange hi-viz
scolding us in the thickest of Norfolk accents.
They can't accept.
Too rubbish for rubbish.
So back it goes into the boot
and back into the garage ready to be
rediscovered again next time,
unlike your will, which after you died,
nobody could apparently find.

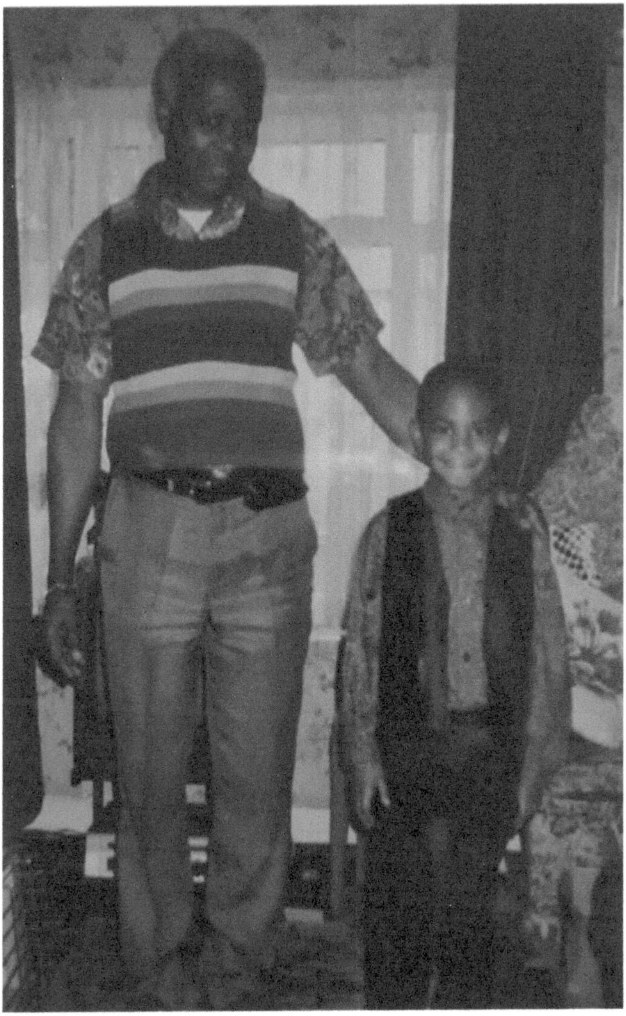

BURGER KING POEM

Wasn't sure how to feel seeing Dad for
the first time since his heart attack and him
asking me to warm up his Burger King.
I should have perhaps been grateful
he came all that way. And I was, in a way.
But he looked even deader than you climbing
the stairs clutching the sweating brown bag.
What's killing him isn't his sweet tooth
or the heart attack he had too young
or even the Chicken Royale or whatever it was.
It's you and nanny dying when you did
and him struggling to find the words
just like he's struggling to catch his breath
shuffling away from me stuffing his burger into his mouth.

HEAVEN

Hope you're not up there watching we wank
and necking two ProPlus for breakfast
and scoffing Cheetos and a can of Coke for lunch
and lying about the books I've read
and driving over the speed limit
and calling someone who can't drive a nonce
and picking the scabs off my shin again
and saying things I shouldn't for banter in the WhatsApp chat
and pissing on the toilet seat
and drinking far too much
and doing that dirty line in that dirty club toilet
and thinking about women I shouldn't
and biting my nails until they bleed
and on dark days when I really should speak to someone

                                                                                cry

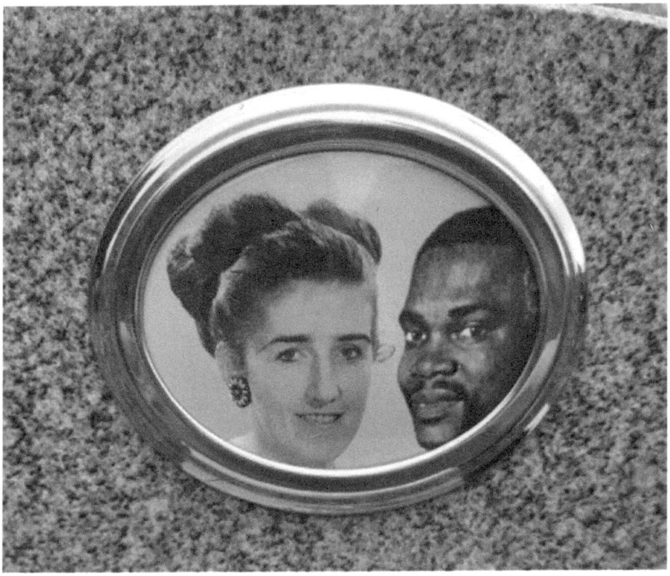

II.
"THE FAMOUS 7A"

The 7A Bus Route

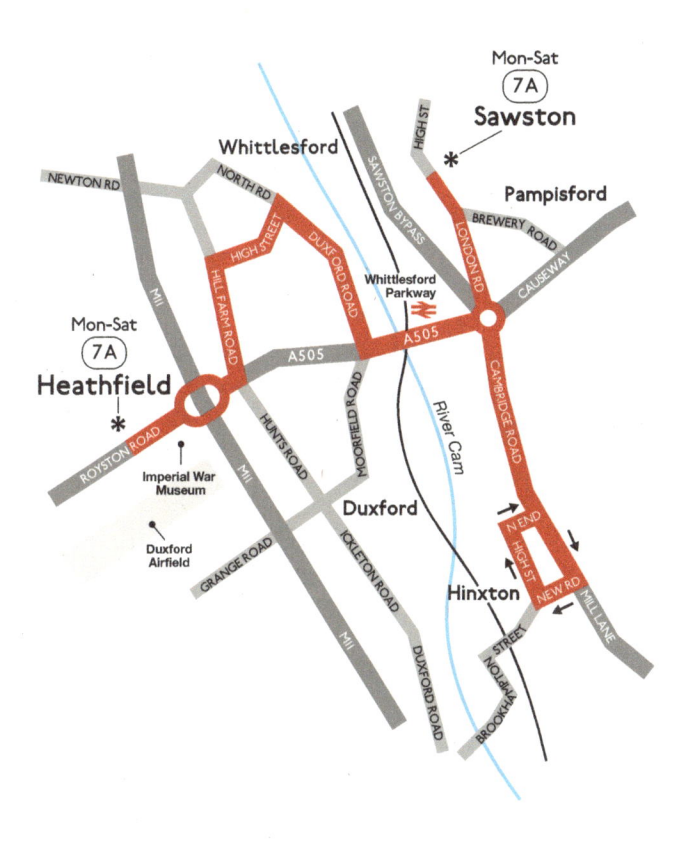

Thanks for joining us.
Our top story - step aboard the bus route
thought to be one of the most expensive in the region
costing the taxpayer £124 per passenger.

The 7A completes a 12-and-a-half-mile loop around
four South Cambridgeshire settlements.
Last year it carried a total of 771 people.
Our political correspondent Ben Schofield took a ride.

HEATHFIELD

Today's driver, Charlie Morley, passed his test in December, a few days after turning 18. He wanted to be a driver "for as long as [he] can remember"
—*BBC News,* January 2024

He should be running riot on the rec
listening to tinny dnb sinking tinnis
twosing a zoot gassing on about lipsing
Gemma from his textiles class
talking tongue piercings and neck tattoos
but instead he's here in Heathfield
embracing the quiet whirr of the ignition
like it's the beginning of a Beethoven.
He only passed his test six months ago
but this morning he's behind the wheel
to pick up his first passenger of the day:
Hello, my darling! he says, opening the doors,
cheery voice older than his eighteen years.
He loves this, all of it, just as it is.

The 7A runs on a 12-mile route in Cambridgeshire linking the Imperial War Museum at Duxford to Whittlesford, Sawston and Hinxton.

IMPERIAL WAR MUSEUM

She's a year short of eighty and this bus
gives her back her independence
but she has to be careful what she says, she says,
it doesn't always turn up, she admits,
looking furtively over her shoulder,
it needs to be reliable, she whispers.
Too often she has to ring someone for a lift
if, like today, she wants to go to the war museum
where they play Vera Lynn in the café.
She's hoping to meet a friend there,
one of very few she has left—remaining players
in the who'll last the longest contest.
Hello, my darling! croaks the driver,
young enough to be her great-grandson.

*The route is one of around twenty
that's been reviewed by the Cambridgeshire and
Peterborough Combined Authority,
meaning the 7A could soon be merged
with a home-to-school service.
It's aiming for subsidised routes to cost no more
than £12 per passenger,
ten times less than the 7A gets.*

*The elected mayor of the area
wants to make big changes to the network.*

DUXFORD

After another long day of meetings and number
crunching, he gets home, pecks his wife on the lips
and snuggles up with his daughter till it's her bedtime.
She doesn't care that's he's the mayor
of Cambridge and Peterborough,
she just wants to watch *In the Night Garden*.
As she drifts off to the soothing squeaks
of Igglepiggle his mind turns to the small
route giving him a big headache.
He knows it's not value for money,
it never was and unless his bus tax
increase is approved he's unsure what the future
holds for the famous 7A. His words.
All he needs now is for this migraine to go away.

Although some people rely on it,
its operator admits it doesn't represent value for money.
It carried 771 passengers last financial year.
Its operator says they've carried fewer in recent months.

WHITTLESFORD PARKWAY

For the very few passengers who use it,
says the owner of A2B Travel, it really is important.
But it needs to be more thought out,
it needs to have a better start and end point
it doesn't run from a high population area
to a high population area,
it doesn't run particularly where
shoppers and commuters want to go
but he's trying his best to make it work,
the route already interworks with the 31
to provide a more cost-effective solution
just like the authority asked for but he's
running out of options and unless something changes soon,
deep down he knows the 7A's days are numbered.

The Cambridgeshire and Peterborough Combined Authority are aiming for subsidised routes to cost no more than £12 per passenger, casting doubt on the route's future and the possible impact on its passengers.

HINXTON

He grew up in Hinxton in the 80s.
Used to take the old Green Line 799
for trips up to Cambridge with his sister
and on one occasion, close to Christmas,
went all the way down to London.
The driver was dressed as Santa.
But the glory days are done.
Now even the 7A, which he hadn't even heard of
till tonight, is on its last legs, he reads
in an online forum somewhere, unable to sleep.
What's happening to this country! he thinks,
furiously two-finger-typing a reply
about the good old days from abroad.
A long way from Hinxton. A distance from it all.

PAMPISFORD

What about the people trying to get somewhere?
Like the student who's got a lecture to attend
or the amateur historian and his wife
trying to make the most of their museum membership
or the football referee with a school game later
or the fella who's recently moved to Pampisford
and doesn't have a car so cycles to Whittlesford
then catches the train to Cambridge for work?
His health is deteriorating so he needs
the 7A to get to his GP up in Sawston.
What about him and all the other residents
residing in this little tucked away village
in the backend of nowhere?
How will they all get to where they need to be?

SAWSTON

The famous 7A? He's never heard of it.
At nearly fifty he's still a Hackney boy at heart.
Murder Mile scar along his cheek
carved into him at eighteen that proves it.
Had reservations at first, moving up here,
being a Black man, East London born and bred,
took the plunge for love and stayed despite
the heartbreak. Needs a break—deserves one.
Athletic and poetic with a wicked sense of humour
but struggles to keep the wolf from the door
or treat his kids to Nandos and new Air Forces.
A man of his many talents should have been someone.
He just wants to feel like the old him again but
it's hard to miss something you didn't know existed.

So what is going to happen with the 7A?
And are you worried about a route in your area?
Scan the QR code on your screen now
to send us a message on WhatsApp
or send us an email.
You can also find us on social media.

Now… people living in a seaside village badly
affected by coastal erosion have been in Downing Street
this morning to demand more protection.

III.
AFTER FRANK

UPPER TULSE HILL

Did you see me?
I was thinking of you
having a Coke in the cold it was your face
I saw on the side of a 415
no it was a 2
I was thinking of you
making annotations reading Beckett
no it was a Shakespeare play
and down at the railway bridge
by the station
as the 432 pulled away in the daylight
towards Upper Tulse Hill
I was thinking of you
and right now I am still

ANGEL

in loving memory of Nassirudeen 'Nass' Osawe

*In the next two minutes, according to eye-witnesses,
all hell broke loose and the area outside The York pub
at Angel looked like a scene from the Wild West*

—*Islington Tribune*, September 2008

just a boy on a bus approaching Angel / heading
West End to buy an Xbox cable / keeping his head
down / minding his own business the way he'd been
conditioned to / had drilled into him from young
/ less than a week away from reaching seventeen /
sketching his way through sixth form / plotting his
escape out of ends to get to uni / he was just about to
get off / but he was being watched / he clocked / he
was just outside The York when things took a turn /
a madness ensued / *all hell broke loose* / he was hoping
it was just some kind of game / he was just a young
black boy buying a cable / that got tangled & now
dangles like a noose

MARRIOTT'S WAY

Ran the Marriott's Way 10k last year, pre-booked
the shuttle bus that takes you back to the start.
From the finish line we drag our tired legs to the bus stop
and wait, while someone in hi-viz regularly reassures
us the bus should be here any minute.

Much later, the little bus is driven to our feet
by a man too old to be behind the wheel. Half way
back to Aylsham he pulls up to take a call,
he's defensive then apologetic then embarrassed.

This year I ran the race again, much slower this time,
and the shuttle bus arrives early and the driver is young
with a nose piercing and my dad's in hospital
with a suspected heart attack and
I'm not sure I have it in me to visit.

CLINGER COURT

you havin a party? bossman asks   it's just a couple of
cans and manomasa   serrano chilli & yucatan honey
  all for me   & as I sink my pre-drinks at mum's
(who looks as sleep-starved as she says
she always feels)   who nicks a crisp with hungry hands
scrunches up her face   winces   says she's got
chicken to cook for dinner later anyway   I take them
back   fold them over   tuck them away
down what I can before the faber party
where I'll keep drinking   forget everyone's name
hope there are plans to go to a good pub   then
a loud club   miss the last train   come the end
of the night   it's a one-way trip to mum's sofa
pan still clean   chicken still defrosting   craving my
crisps   but they're not where I left them
then I spot   the empty packet   in the bin
        unfurling

HIGHBURY BARN (THE 263 HAS BEEN EXTENDED!)

The 263 has been extended!
We were trotting along and suddenly
spotting second-hand furniture we amended
our route and crossed over in such a hurry
it was hot and you said you liked it hot
but I don't really but just pretended
and suddenly I see the sign on the bus stop
THE 263 HAS BEEN EXTENDED!
It's been extended before to Holloway
It's been extended further to Highbury
I've acted perfectly excited on such a day
and still passersby can't take their eyes off me
like the TfL font you're the diamond of my *i*
oh I love you let's go give this extension a try

WHY I AM NOT A BUS DRIVER

I am not a bus driver, I am a writer. Why?
I think I would rather be a bus driver, but I am not.
Well, for instance, I see the 47 pull in and I
get on from the Catford Garage stop.
I get on; I stay on. I look out. "**47 to Shoreditch**"
The journey is going on, and the places go by, passengers leave.
The route is finished. It's too much. All of it.
All that's left are people living beyond their means.

But me? One day I am thinking about the future: you.
I write a line about you. Pretty soon, it is a whole page of words,
Not lines. There could be so much more, of you too,
of how lovely you are and life and days that go by like birds.
My poem is finished. It's forty poems, which I call
WHY I AM NOT A BUS DRIVER but aren't about buses at all.

ACKNOWLEDGEMENTS

I am immensely grateful to my editor at Bad Betty Press, Amy Acre, for her attentiveness, wisdom and kindness in getting this into shape (the idea for this collection began when I was still a teenager!). Jake Wild Hall, also of Bad Betty, for his positivity and support. Philippa Sitters, my agent, for her belief in me and this collection from day one. Kayleigh Campbell for her thorough and generous editorial advice. Lewis Buxton for having an early look and urging me to have fun with the rules. Maks Julikovs for the 7A bus route design. All my close friends and family. Zadie for the joy. Elisabeth, always, for her love.

The inspiration for "The Famous 7A" section is thanks to Ben Schofield and BBC Look East for covering the story in January 2024.

The poem 'Notting Hill' was originally published as 'These Same Streets' in *Part of a Story That Started Before Me* by Penguin in 2023.

'Why I Am Not a Bus Driver was written in response to Frank O'Hara's 'Why I Am Not a Painter'.

'Highbury Barn (the 263 has been extended!)' was written in response to Frank O'Hara's 'Poem (Lana Turner has collapsed!)'.

'Upper Tulse Hill' was written in response to Frank O'Hara's 'Song (Did you see me walking by the Buick Repairs?)'.

All photos courtesy of the author and his family.